Ada Lovelace

Published in the United States of America by Cherry Lake Publishing
Ann Arbor, Michigan
www.cherrylakepublishing.com

Content Adviser: Ryan Emery Hughes, Doctoral Student, School of Education, University of Michigan
Reading Adviser: Marla Conn MS, Ed., Literacy specialist, Read-Ability, Inc.
Book Design: Jennifer Wahi
Illustrator: Jeff Bane

Photo Credits: © Samot/Shutterstock, 5; © Wikimedia, 7; © Georgios Kollidas/Shutterstock, 9; © Charles Hayter, 11; © Wikimedia, 13, 22; © Samuel Lawrence, 15; © Margaret Sarah Carpenter, 17, 23; © Alfred Edward Chalon, 19; © Henry Phillips, 21; Cover, 6, 12, 18, Jeff Bane; Various frames throughout, © Shutterstock Images

Library of Congress Cataloging-in-Publication Data

Names: Loh-Hagan, Virginia, author. | Bane, Jeff, 1957- illustrator.
Title: Ada Lovelace / by Virginia Loh-Hagan ; [illustrator, Jeff Bane].
Other titles: My itty-bitty bio.
Description: Ann Arbor, MI : Cherry Lake Publishing, [2018] | Series: My itty-bitty bio | Audience: K to grade 3. | Includes index.
Identifiers: LCCN 2017031206| ISBN 9781534107168 (hardcover) | ISBN 9781534108158 (pbk.) | ISBN 9781534109148 (pdf) | ISBN 9781534120136 (hosted ebook)
Subjects: LCSH: Lovelace, Ada King, Countess of, 1815-1852--Juvenile literature. | Women mathematicians--Great Britain--Biography--Juvenile literature. | Women computer programmers--Great Britain--Biography--Juvenile literature. | Computers--History--19th century.
Classification: LCC QA29.L72 L64 2018 | DDC 510.92 [B] --dc23
LC record available at https://lccn.loc.gov/2017031206

Printed in the United States of America
Corporate Graphics

JANUARY 2018

About the author: Dr. Virginia Loh-Hagan is an author, university professor, former classroom teacher, and curriculum designer. Like Ada, she had a strange childhood. She lives in San Diego with her very tall husband and very naughty dogs. To learn more about her, visit: www.virginialoh.com

About the illustrator: Jeff Bane and his two business partners own a studio along the American River in Folsom, California, home of the 1849 Gold Rush. When Jeff's not sketching or illustrating for clients, he's either swimming or kayaking in the river to relax.

I was born in London. It was 1815.

I loved math. Only boys learned math. But that didn't stop me.

What do you want to learn?

My father was Lord Byron.
He was a **poet**.

He left after I was born. My mother hired **tutors** to teach me math.

I had great ideas. I wanted to fly. I studied birds.

I made myself wings. I was 12.

Do you have any great ideas?

I met Charles Babbage. I was 18. He studied math. He invented the **computer**.

I was smart. I helped spread Babbage's work. I added notes to help people understand.

I invented the first computer **program**.

Babbage's computer did math.
Mine used math to do things.
I used numbers as **codes**.

What do you do on the computer?

I died in 1852. I lived before women were allowed to study freely.

But I dreamed big. My ideas were for the future.

What would you like to ask me?

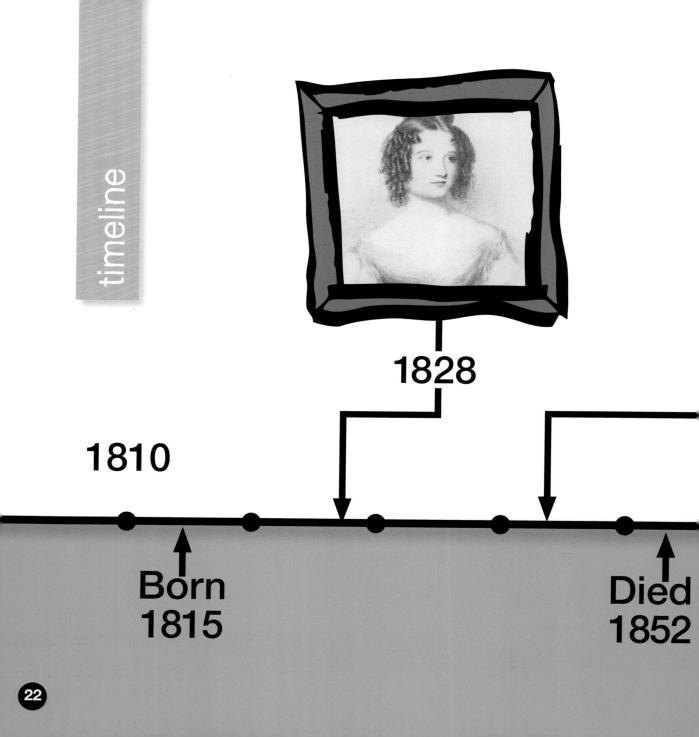

1828

1810

Born
1815

Died
1852

1843

1910

glossary

codes (KOHDZ) systems of words or numbers that tell a computer how to do something

computer (kuhm-PYOO-tur) a machine that can do really hard math problems

poet (POH-it) a person who writes poems

program (PROH-gram) a language that tells computers what to do

tutors (TOO-turz) people who teach one student at a time away from school

index